EASY NUTELLA COOKBOOK

50 Unique and Easy Nutella Recipes

2ND EDITION

By
Chef Maggie Chow
Copyright © 2015 by Saxonberg Associates
All rights reserved

Published by
BookSumo, a division of Saxonberg Associates
http://www.booksumo.com/

Stay To the End of the Cookbook and Receive....

I really appreciate when people, take the time to read all of my recipes.

So, as a gift for reading this entire cookbook you will receive a **massive collection of special recipes.**

Read to the end of this cookbook and get my *Easy Specialty Cookbook Box Set for FREE*!

This box set includes the following:

1. *Easy Sushi Cookbook*

2. ***Easy Dump Dinner Cookbook***
3. ***Easy Beans Cookbook***

Remember this box set is about **EASY** cooking.

In the ***Easy Sushi Cookbook*** you will learn the easiest methods to prepare almost every type of Japanese Sushi i.e. *California Rolls, the Perfect Sushi Rice, Crab Rolls, Osaka Style Sushi*, and so many others.

Then we go on to *Dump Dinners*. Nothing can be easier than a Dump Dinner. In the ***Easy Dump Dinner Cookbook*** we will learn how to master our slow cookers and make some amazingly unique dinners that will take almost **no *effort***.

Finally in the ***Easy Beans Cookbook*** we tackle one of my favorite side dishes: Beans. There are so many delicious ways to make Baked Beans and Bean Salads that I had to share them.

So stay till the end and then keep on cooking with my *Easy Specialty Cookbook Box Set*!

About the Author.

Maggie Chow is the author and creator of your favorite *Easy Cookbooks* and *The Effortless Chef Series*. Maggie is a lover of all things related to food. Maggie loves nothing more than finding new recipes, trying them out, and then making them her own, by adding or removing ingredients, tweaking cooking times, and anything to make the recipe not only taste better, but be easier to cook!

For a complete listing of all my books please see my author page.

INTRODUCTION

Welcome to *The Effortless Chef Series*! Thank you for taking the time to download the *Easy Nutella Cookbook*. Come take a journey with me into the delights of easy cooking. The point of this cookbook and all my cookbooks is to exemplify the effortless nature of cooking simply.

In this book we focus on Nutella. You will find mostly recipes for snacks and desserts as this is Nutella's best purpose. You will find that even though the recipes are simple, the taste of the dishes is quite amazing.

So will you join me in an adventure of simple cooking? If the answer is yes (and I hope it is) please consult the table of contents to find the dishes you are most interested in. Once you are ready jump right in and start cooking.

— Chef Maggie Chow

TABLE OF CONTENTS

Stay To the End of the Cookbook and Receive.................... 2
About the Author.................. 5
Introduction......................... 7
Table of Contents 8
Legal Notes.......................... 12
   A Pie of Peanut Butter and Nutella . 13
   Grilled Pineapple Enhanced............ 16
   A Peanut Butter and Chocolate Pie Which Requires No Baking 18
   Hazelnut Roll 21
   Super Easy Peanut Butter Cups....... 24
   A Pizza Topped with Bananas and Nutella 27
   Nutella Chow-Chow 29
   Easy Hazelnut Cookies 32

French Toast Enhanced 35
Mug Cake Nutella I 38
Nutella Popsicles 41
Very Easy Nutella Cheesecake 43
Hot Chocolate Enhanced 45
Nutella Cups 47
Mug Cake Nutella II 49
Nutella Ice Pops II 51
Nutella Roll Up 53
Midsummer Nutella Dip 55
Coconut Pops Enhanced 57
Classical Nutella Smoothie 59
Super-Easy Nutella Cookies 61
Enhanced No-Bake Pie 63
Cinnamon Nutella No-Bake Cookies 65
Nutella Smores Done Right 68
Microwave Nutella Cake 70
Graham Crackers Re-Imagined 72
Nutella Frosting 74
Broomstick Dip 76

Chocolate-Cinnamon Dip 78
Banana Cake 81
Delightful Nutella Sandwich 84
Chocolate Spread II 86
Peanut Butter Re-Imagined 88
Nutella Pudding 91
Coffee Enhanced 93
Maggie's Homemade Granola Crisps
.... 95
Toast from France 98
Choco Cookies 101
Hazelnut Puff Pastry Rolls 104
No-Bake Hazelnut Oat Bars 107
Upstate New York Style Crepes 110
Pretzel Cookies 114
Easy Smores 117
Sweet Cookies 120
Maggie's Favorite Hazelnut Cupcakes
.... 123
Truffle and Hazelnut Desserts 126
Pancakes from Denmark 129

Strawberry Hazelnut Bark............. 132

Two Times Chocolate Cookies....... 135

Hazelnut Peanut Butter Sandwiches 138

THANKS FOR READING! NOW LET'S TRY SOME **SUSHI** AND **DUMP DINNERS**.... 140

Come On... 142

Let's Be Friends :)............................ 142

About The Publisher......................... 143

Can I Ask A Favour? 144

INTERESTED IN OTHER EASY COOKBOOKS?................................... 145

LEGAL NOTES

ALL RIGHTS RESERVED. NO PART OF THIS BOOK MAY BE REPRODUCED OR TRANSMITTED IN ANY FORM OR BY ANY MEANS. PHOTOCOPYING, POSTING ONLINE, AND / OR DIGITAL COPYING IS STRICTLY PROHIBITED UNLESS WRITTEN PERMISSION IS GRANTED BY THE BOOK'S PUBLISHING COMPANY. LIMITED USE OF THE BOOK'S TEXT IS PERMITTED FOR USE IN REVIEWS WRITTEN FOR THE PUBLIC AND/OR PUBLIC DOMAIN.

A Pie of Peanut Butter and Nutella

Ingredients

- 8 ounces reduced-fat cream cheese, softened
- 1/2 cup peanut butter
- 1/2 cup chocolate-hazelnut spread (such as Nutella®)
- 1/4 cup agave syrup
- 1/4 cup honey
- 1 egg
- 1 tsp vanilla extract
- 1/2 tsp baking soda
- 1/4 tsp sea salt

Directions

- At first, preheat your oven to 350 degrees F before doing anything else.
- Whisk cream cheese, chocolate-hazelnut spread, honey, egg, peanut butter, vanilla extract, baking soda, agave syrup and sea

salt in a bowl very thoroughly until you see that a dough is formed.
- Drop this dough into the baking dish with the help of a spoon.
- Now bake this in the preheated oven for about 12 minutes.
- Let it cool for three minutes before serving.
- Enjoy.

Serving: 4 dozen

Timing Information:

Preparation	Cooking	Total Time
15 mins	15 mins	50 mins

Nutritional Information:

Calories	52 kcal
Carbohydrates	5.2 g
Cholesterol	7 mg
Fat	3 g
Fiber	0.2 g
Protein	1.5 g
Sodium	53 mg

* Percent Daily Values are based on a 2,000 calorie diet.

Grilled Pineapple Enhanced

Ingredients

- 1/2 cup chocolate-hazelnut spread (such as Nutella®)
- 1/4 cup milk
- 1/2 fresh pineapple, peeled and cored
- 1/4 cup walnuts

Directions

- At first you need to set a grill to medium heat and put some oil before starting anything else.
- Heat up the mixture of chocolate hazelnut spread and milk in a saucepan until you see that the spread has melted.
- Cook pineapple on the preheated grill for about 5 minutes on each side before pouring the chocolate mixture over it in a serving dish.
- Serve.

Serving: 4

Timing Information:

Preparation	Cooking	Total Time
10 mins	10 mins	20 mins

Nutritional Information:

Calories	246 kcal
Carbohydrates	28.5 g
Cholesterol	1 mg
Fat	14.3 g
Fiber	1.3 g
Protein	4 g
Sodium	37 mg

* Percent Daily Values are based on a 2,000 calorie diet.

A Peanut Butter and Chocolate Pie Which Requires No Baking

Ingredients

- 3/4 cup chocolate-hazelnut spread (such as Nutella®)
- 1 (9 inch) prepared graham cracker crust
- 1 3/4 cups heavy whipping cream
- 3/4 cup peanut butter
- 1/2 cup cream cheese, softened
- 1/4 cup sweetened condensed milk

Directions

- Refrigerate graham cracker crust for about 30 minutes after spreading chocolate hazelnut over it.
- With the help of an electric mixer, beat cream until you see that the required smoothness is achieved

before transferring it to a bowl and setting it aside for later use.
- Whish peanut butter, condensed milk and cream cheese together in a bowl until you see that the required smoothness is achieved before adding the remaining whipped cream.
- Also add some whipped cream over it before refrigerating it for at least four full hours.

Serving: 4

Timing Information:

Preparation	Cooking	Total Time
15 mins		4 hrs 30 mins

Nutritional Information:

Calories	894 kcal
Carbohydrates	60.7 g
Cholesterol	121 mg
Fat	68.7 g
Fiber	2.5 g
Protein	15.7 g
Sodium	505 mg

* Percent Daily Values are based on a 2,000 calorie diet.

Hazelnut Roll

Ingredients

Rolls:

- 3 cups bread flour
- 1 cup milk
- 5 tbsps white sugar
- 1/4 cup butter, melted
- 1 egg
- 2 1/4 tsps instant yeast
- 1 1/2 tsps salt

Filling:

- 2 tbsps butter, softened
- 1 cup chocolate-hazelnut spread (such as Nutella®)
- 1/2 cup coarsely chopped hazelnuts

Directions

- At first, preheat your oven to 350 degrees F before doing anything else.

- Add a mixture of bread flour, salt, milk, melted butter, yeast, white sugar and eggs into the bread machine, and start it after selecting the dough cycle.
- Roll this dough over a floured surface into large sized rectangles before adding butter and chocolate hazelnut spread over it.
- Add some hazelnuts and then roll it around the filling before cutting into 12 even sized parts.
- Place them in the baking dish.
- Now bake this in the preheated oven for about 25 minutes.

Serving: 12

Timing Information:

Preparation	Cooking	Total Time
45 mins	25 mins	1 hr 10 mins

Nutritional Information:

Calories	350 kcal
Carbohydrates	44.8 g
Cholesterol	32 mg
Fat	16.1 g
Fiber	1.4 g
Protein	7.7 g
Sodium	367 mg

* Percent Daily Values are based on a 2,000 calorie diet.

Super Easy Peanut Butter Cups

Ingredients

Peanut Butter Layer:

- 3/4 cup peanut butter
- 2 tbsps coconut oil, melted
- 1 tbsp raw honey

Chocolate Layer:

- 1/2 cup chocolate-hazelnut spread (such as Nutella®), or more to taste
- 1/4 cup raw cocoa powder
- 1/4 cup coconut oil, melted
- 1 tbsp raw honey
- 1 tbsp peanut butter
- 1 packet stevia powder

Directions

- Mix 3/4 cup peanut butter, 1 tbsp honey and 2 tbsps coconut oil in a medium sized bowl, and in a

separate bowl, combine chocolate hazelnut spread, 1/4 cup coconut oil, 1 tbsp honey, 1 tbsp peanut butter, cocoa powder and stevia powder.
- Pour peanut butter mixture into muffin cups of your choice before topping each cup with the chocolate mixture.
- Refrigerate or freeze before serving.

Serving: 12

Timing Information:

Preparation	Cooking	Total Time
15 mins	1 hr	1 hr 15 mins

Nutritional Information:

Calories	231 kcal
Carbohydrates	13.7 g
Cholesterol	0 mg
Fat	19.1 g
Fiber	1.7 g
Protein	5.4 g
Sodium	91 mg

* Percent Daily Values are based on a 2,000 calorie diet.

A Pizza Topped with Bananas and Nutella

Ingredients

- 1/2 cup chocolate-hazelnut spread (such as Nutella®), or to taste
- 1 large tortilla
- 1 banana, cut into 1/4-inch-thick slices

Directions

- Put hazelnut chocolate spread over a tortilla evenly before spreading banana slices on top of it.
- Cook tortilla over high heat for about 5 minutes or until you see that it is crispy.
- Allow it to cool for four minutes before cutting it into four equal slices.
- Serve.

Serving: 4

Timing Information:

Preparation	Cooking	Total Time
5 mins	5 mins	15 mins

Nutritional Information:

Calories	249 kcal
Carbohydrates	36 g
Cholesterol	0 mg
Fat	10.6 g
Fiber	1.4 g
Protein	4 g
Sodium	158 mg

* Percent Daily Values are based on a 2,000 calorie diet.

Nutella Chow-Chow

Ingredients

- 1 (11 ounce) package milk chocolate chips
- 1/2 cup chocolate-hazelnut spread (such as Nutella®)
- 8 cups bite-size corn square cereal (such as Corn Chex®)
- 1 1/2 cups confectioners' sugar

Directions

- Melt down a mixture of chocolate hazelnut spread and chocolate chips over high heat before adding cereal and mixing it thoroughly.
- Now transfer this cereal mixture to a bag and shake it well after adding confectioners' sugar into it.
- Transfer this chow-chow to a container that is airtight.
- Enjoy your chow-chow.

NOTE: Chow-chow should be thought of as a popcorn replacement.

Serving: 8

Timing Information:

Preparation	Cooking	Total Time
10 mins	5 mins	15 mins

Nutritional Information:

Calories	233 kcal
Carbohydrates	41.4 g
Cholesterol	0 mg
Fat	8.3 g
Fiber	1.7 g
Protein	2.3 g
Sodium	150 mg

* Percent Daily Values are based on a 2,000 calorie diet.

Easy Hazelnut Cookies

Ingredients

- 1 sheet frozen puff pastry, thawed
- 1 cup chocolate-hazelnut spread (such as Nutella®)
- 1/3 cup finely chopped, roasted hazelnuts

Directions

- Put chocolate hazelnut spread and hazelnuts evenly over puff pastry.
- Take the long edge and roll it around the filling until you reach the middle, and do the same with the other long edge to meet the first roll in the middle.
- Refrigerate it for at least thirty minutes before you do anything else.
- Set your oven at 450 degrees F.
- Take out the pastry and cut it into slices that are ¾ inch approx.

- Put these slices in the preheated oven over baking sheet and bake it for 7 minutes before turning it and baking it for another 5 minutes.
- Serve.

Serving: 12

Timing Information:

Preparation	Cooking	Total Time
15 mins	10 mins	55 mins

Nutritional Information:

Calories	237 kcal
Carbohydrates	22.3 g
Cholesterol	0 mg
Fat	15.6 g
Fiber	0.6 g
Protein	3.3 g
Sodium	70 mg

* Percent Daily Values are based on a 2,000 calorie diet.

FRENCH TOAST ENHANCED

Ingredients

- 1/4 cup chocolate-hazelnut spread (such as Nutella®)
- 4 slices bread
- 1 banana, sliced
- 1/4 cup chocolate milk
- 2 eggs, beaten
- 1 tbsp vanilla extract
- 1/2 tsp ground cinnamon
- 2 tbsps butter

Directions

- Put chocolate hazelnut spread on one side of two bread slices before topping them with banana slices.
- Place the remaining bread slices on top to form two sandwiches.
- Mix cinnamon, chocolate milk, vanilla extract and eggs in a medium sized bowl and dip those

sandwiches in it completely to get completely coated.
- Cook these sandwiches over low heat in hot butter for about 6 minutes each side.
- Serve.

Serving: 2

Timing Information:

Preparation	Cooking	Total Time
15 mins	10 mins	25 mins

Nutritional Information:

Calories	563 kcal
Carbohydrates	63.1 g
Cholesterol	219 mg
Fat	28 g
Fiber	3 g
Protein	13.9 g
Sodium	552 mg

* Percent Daily Values are based on a 2,000 calorie diet.

Mug Cake Nutella I

Ingredients

- 2 tbsps all-purpose flour
- 2 tbsps coconut flour
- 1 tbsp cocoa powder
- 1/4 tsp baking powder
- 3 1/2 tbsps almond milk, divided
- 1/2 tsp vanilla extract
- 3 tbsps chocolate-hazelnut spread (such as Nutella®)

Directions

- Combine coconut flour, cocoa powder, all-purpose flour and baking powder in a medium sized bowl before adding 3 tbsps almond milk, Nutella®, vanilla extract and 1/2 tbsp milk one by one into the flour mixture, while stirring continuously in that time.
- Pour this mixture into a mug and cook this in the microwave for about one minutes before letting

it stand as it is for five seconds and cooking it again for 30 seconds more in the microwave oven.
- Let it cool before serving.

Serving: 1

Timing Information:

Preparation	Cooking	Total Time
5 mins	2 mins	12 mins

Nutritional Information:

Calories	450 kcal
Carbohydrates	65.8 g
Cholesterol	0 mg
Fat	18 g
Fiber	14.4 g
Protein	9.9 g
Sodium	203 mg

* Percent Daily Values are based on a 2,000 calorie diet.

Nutella Popsicles

Ingredients

- 6 tbsps chocolate-hazelnut spread (such as Nutella)
- 1 cup milk
- 2 cups heavy whipping cream

Directions

- Mix cream, chocolate hazelnut and milk together in a bowl before putting it in the microwave oven for 2 minutes to melt down the hazelnut while stirring every 30 seconds.
- Pour this mixture in ice pop molds and freeze it for about 4 hours.

Servings: 8

Timing Information:

Preparation	Cooking	Total Time
10 mins	5 min	3 hrs 15 mins

Nutritional Information:

Calories	281 kcal
Carbohydrates	10.2 g
Cholesterol	62 mg
Fat	40.2 g
Protein	84 g
Sodium	24 mg

* Percent Daily Values are based on a 2,000 calorie diet.

Very Easy Nutella Cheesecake

Ingredients

- 2 (8 ounce) packages cream cheese, room temperature
- 1/2 cup white sugar
- 1 (13 ounce) jar chocolate-hazelnut spread, such as Nutella
- 1/4 tsp vanilla extract
- 1 (9 inch) prepared graham cracker crust

Directions

- Take out a large bowl and mix cream, sugar, Nutella and vanilla before putting it in a freezer for about 4 hours.
- Serve.

Servings: 19 inch cake

Timing Information:

Preparation	Cooking	Total Time
10 mins		4 hrs 10 mins

Nutritional Information:

Calories	627 kcal
Carbohydrates	61.4 g
Cholesterol	62 mg
Fat	40.2 g
Protein	8.4 g
Sodium	380 mg

* Percent Daily Values are based on a 2,000 calorie diet.

HOT CHOCOLATE ENHANCED

Ingredients

- 3/4 cup hazelnut liqueur (such as Frangelico)
- 1 (13 ounce) jar chocolate-hazelnut spread (such as Nutella)
- 1 quart half-and-half

Directions

- Put half and half to low heat in a saucepan and add chocolate hazelnut spread.
- Cook for about 10 minutes and just before serving add hazelnut liqueur.

Servings: 8

Timing Information:

Preparation	Cooking	Total Time
10 mins	10 mins	20 mins

Nutritional Information:

Calories	627 kcal
Carbohydrates	61.4 g
Cholesterol	62 mg
Fat	40.2 g
Protein	8.4 g
Sodium	380 mg

* Percent Daily Values are based on a 2,000 calorie diet.

Nutella Cups

Ingredients

- 2 (8 ounce) packages refrigerated crescent rolls
- 2 ripe bananas, sliced
- 12 tbsps chocolate-hazelnut spread (such as Nutella), or more to taste
- 1 tsp confectioners' sugar, or to taste

Directions

- First, preheat your oven to 375 degrees before continuing.
- Put 2 crescent roll triangles into muffin cups and fill these cups with banana slices and chocolate hazelnut over the banana slices.
- Now bake this for about 13 minutes or until golden brown and serve.

Servings: 12

Timing Information:

Preparation	Cooking	Total Time
10 mins	10 mins	20 mins

Nutritional Information:

Calories	245 kcal
Carbohydrates	28.9 g
Cholesterol	0 mg
Fat	12.6 g
Protein	3.9 g
Sodium	309 mg

* Percent Daily Values are based on a 2,000 calorie diet.

Mug Cake Nutella II

Ingredients

- 1/4 cup self-rising flour
- 1/4 cup white sugar
- 1 egg, beaten
- 3 tbsps cocoa powder
- 3 tbsps chocolate-hazelnut spread (such as Nutella)
- 3 tbsps milk
- 3 tbsps vegetable oil

Directions

- Mix all the ingredients mentioned in a coffee mug with a fork until you find it smooth.
- Cook this in the microwave oven for about 3 minutes.
- Enjoy.

Servings: 12

Timing Information:

Preparation	Cooking	Total Time
10 mins	3 mins	13 mins

Nutritional Information:

Calories	475 kcal
Carbohydrates	113g
Cholesterol	190 mg
Fat	62.8 g
Protein	17.1 g
Sodium	534 mg

* Percent Daily Values are based on a 2,000 calorie diet.

Nutella Ice Pops II

Ingredients

- 1 cup whipped cream
- 1/2 cup whole milk
- 1/4 cup chocolate-hazelnut spread (such as Nutella)

Directions

- Put all the ingredients mentioned into a blender and blend it for about 2 minutes.
- Now pour this mixture into ice pop molds and place them in your freezer for about 3 hours to get solid.

Servings: 8

Timing Information:

Preparation	Cooking	Total Time
10 mins		3 hr 10 mins

Nutritional Information:

Calories	137 kcal
Carbohydrates	12.8g
Cholesterol	14 mg
Fat	8.8 g
Protein	2.5 g
Sodium	47 mg

* Percent Daily Values are based on a 2,000 calorie diet.

Nutella Roll Up

Ingredients

- 1 tortilla
- 1/4 cup chocolate-hazelnut spread (such as Nutella)
- 1 small banana

Directions

- Put chocolate spread on the corners of a tortilla that is warmed in the microwave oven for 10 seconds and fold it around the banana slice.
- Cut it into half and serve.

Servings: 2

Timing Information:

Preparation	Cooking	Total Time
5 mins		5 mins

Nutritional Information:

Calories	317 kcal
Carbohydrates	49g
Cholesterol	0 mg
Fat	11.9 g
Protein	5.5 g
Sodium	259 mg

* Percent Daily Values are based on a 2,000 calorie diet.

Midsummer Nutella Dip

Ingredients

- 5 tbsps chocolate-hazelnut spread (such as Nutella)
- 2 tbsps milk
- 1 tsp honey
- 1/4 tsp vanilla extract

Directions

- Mix all the ingredients mentioned and put them to heat in the microwave for about 1 minute.
- Let it cool for 2 minutes before serving.

Servings: 4

Timing Information:

Preparation	Cooking	Total Time
1 mins		8 mins

Nutritional Information:

Calories	110 kcal
Carbohydrates	13.8g
Cholesterol	< 1 mg
Fat	5.8 g
Protein	1.5 g
Sodium	22 mg

* Percent Daily Values are based on a 2,000 calorie diet.

Coconut Pops Enhanced

Ingredients

- 1 (14 ounce) can coconut cream
- 1/2 cup chocolate-hazelnut spread (such as Nutella), or more to taste

Directions

- Whisk coconut cream until smooth and add chocolate hazelnut spread and mix it well.
- Pour this mixture into ice-pop molds and let it freeze for about 4 hours.
- Serve

Servings: 6

Timing Information:

Preparation	Cooking	Total Time
5 mins	10 mins	4 h 5 m

Nutritional Information:

Calories	340 kcal
Carbohydrates	47.4g
Cholesterol	0 mg
Fat	16.6 g
Protein	2.1 g
Sodium	44 mg

* Percent Daily Values are based on a 2,000 calorie diet.

Classical Nutella Smoothie

Ingredients

- 6 fluid ounces low-fat milk
- 6 ounces plain fat-free Greek yogurt
- 1 banana, sliced
- 4 fresh strawberries
- 2 tbsps chocolate-hazelnut spread (such as Nutella)

Directions

- Put all the ingredients mentioned into blender and blend until smooth.

Servings: 1

Timing Information:

Preparation	Cooking	Total Time
10 mins		10 mins

Nutritional Information:

Calories	457 kcal
Carbohydrates	67.4g
Cholesterol	7 mg
Fat	11.4 g
Protein	24.9 g
Sodium	190 mg

* Percent Daily Values are based on a 2,000 calorie diet.

Super-Easy Nutella Cookies

Ingredients

- 1 cup all-purpose flour
- 2 tbsps white sugar
- 2 eggs
- 1/4 cup chocolate-hazelnut spread (such as Nutella)

Directions

- First, preheat your oven to 350 degrees F before continuing.
- Combine flour and sugar together in a medium sized bowl and add eggs and mix thoroughly.
- Now add chocolate hazelnut spread and place into a baking sheet by making several balls and pressing them.
- Bake this in the preheated oven for about 25 minutes.
- Let it cool down and serve.

Servings: 6

Timing Information:

Preparation	Cooking	Total Time
10 mins	20 mins	30 mins

Nutritional Information:

Calories	169 kcal
Carbohydrates	26.5g
Cholesterol	62 mg
Fat	4.9 g
Protein	4.9 g
Sodium	34 mg

* Percent Daily Values are based on a 2,000 calorie diet.

Enhanced No-Bake Pie

Ingredients

- 1 (13 ounce) jar chocolate-hazelnut spread (such as Nutella), divided
- 1 (9 inch) prepared graham cracker crust
- 1 (8 ounce) package cream cheese, softened
- 1 (8 ounce) container frozen whipped topping, thawed

Directions

- Put a quarter cup of chocolate hazelnut spread over graham cracker crust.
- Now whish hazelnut spread and some cream cheese in some bowl until you find it smooth and add whipped topping before putting this mixture over the crust.
- Put the mixture in the refrigerator for about 4 hours.
- Enjoy.

Servings: 6

Timing Information:

Preparation	Cooking	Total Time
10 mins		4 hr 20 mins

Nutritional Information:

Calories	759 kcal
Carbohydrates	72.8g
Cholesterol	41 mg
Fat	50 g
Protein	8.9 g
Sodium	406 mg

* Percent Daily Values are based on a 2,000 calorie diet.

Cinnamon Nutella No-Bake Cookies

Ingredients

- 2 cups white sugar
- 1/2 cup butter
- 1/2 cup milk
- 1 (10 ounce) package cinnamon chips
- 1/2 cup chocolate-hazelnut spread (such as Nutella)
- 3 cups old-fashioned rolled oats

Directions

- Put some parchment paper over a baking sheet and mix sugar, milk, and butter in a small saucepan and cook for about 2 minutes.
- After removing this saucepan from the heat, add cinnamon chips, hazelnut spread, and some oats.
- Now place a cookie sized mixture into a baking sheet and allow it to cool down.

- Serve.

Servings: 6

Timing Information:

Preparation	Cooking	Total Time
10 mins	5 mins	15 mins

Nutritional Information:

Calories	152 kcal
Carbohydrates	22.7g
Cholesterol	7 mg
Fat	22.7g
Protein	1.9 g
Sodium	40 mg

* Percent Daily Values are based on a 2,000 calorie diet.

Nutella Smores Done Right

Ingredients

- 4 whole graham crackers, broken into two square halves
- 2 tbsps chocolate-hazelnut spread (such as Nutella)
- 2 tbsps marshmallow cream

Directions

- Put half a tsp of hazelnut spread over four graham cracker halves and half tsp marshmallow cream over the remaining 3 cracker halves.
- Now take one marshmallow half, and one hazelnut spread topped half, and press together.
- Do this for all crackers to get multiple sets and serve.

Servings: 4

Timing Information:

Preparation	Cooking	Total Time
10 mins		20 mins

Nutritional Information:

Calories	79 kcal
Carbohydrates	12.5g
Cholesterol	0 mg
Fat	3 g
Protein	1 g
Sodium	52 mg

* Percent Daily Values are based on a 2,000 calorie diet.

Microwave Nutella Cake

Ingredients

- 1/4 cup self-rising flour
- 1/4 cup white sugar
- 1 egg
- 3 tbsps vegetable oil
- 3 tbsps milk
- 2 tbsps unsweetened cocoa powder, or more to taste
- 2 tbsps chocolate-hazelnut spread (such as Nutella), or more to taste
- 1/2 tsp salt
- 1/2 tsp vanilla extract

Directions

- Put all the ingredients mentioned into a large sized mug and whisk it until smooth.
- Now cook this in a microwave oven for about 2 minutes or until the cake has risen.
- Serve.

Servings: 2

Timing Information:

Preparation	Cooking	Total Time
10 mins	5 mins	15 mins

Nutritional Information:

Calories	475 kcal
Carbohydrates	50.4g
Cholesterol	95 mg
Fat	28.8 g
Protein	7.5 g
Sodium	840 mg

* Percent Daily Values are based on a 2,000 calorie diet.

Graham Crackers Re-Imagined

Ingredients

- 30 sliced fresh strawberries
- 1 (7 ounce) can whipped cream
- 1 (13 ounce) jar chocolate-hazelnut spread (such as Nutella)
- 30 fresh blueberries
- 1 (14.4 ounce) package mini graham crackers

Directions

- First, cut the bottom part of each strawberry and create a hole in each of them from the top.
- Now put whipped cream and hazelnut spread into this hole, and top this with one blueberry.
- Cover with a graham cracker before serving.
- Enjoy.

Servings: 30

Timing Information:

Preparation	Cooking	Total Time
20 mins		20 mins

Nutritional Information:

Calories	144 kcal
Carbohydrates	20.3g
Cholesterol	5 mg
Fat	6.4 g
Protein	2.1 g
Sodium	103 mg

* Percent Daily Values are based on a 2,000 calorie diet.

Nutella Frosting

Ingredients

- 1 (16 ounce) can prepared chocolate frosting
- 3/4 cup chocolate-hazelnut spread (such as Nutella)
- 3/4 cup confectioners' sugar
- 1 tsp vanilla extract

Directions

- Put all the ingredients mentioned into a blender and blend for about 2 minutes or until smooth.
- Serve.

NOTE: Use as a topping for cakes, cookies, and even tortillas.

Servings: 22

Timing Information:

Preparation	Cooking	Total Time
5 mins		5 mins

Nutritional Information:

Calories	144 kcal
Carbohydrates	20.3g
Cholesterol	0 mg
Fat	6.4 g
Protein	2.1 g
Sodium	103 mg

* Percent Daily Values are based on a 2,000 calorie diet.

Broomstick Dip

Ingredients

- 1 cup smooth peanut butter
- 1 cup chocolate-hazelnut spread (such as Nutella)
- 1/2 cup oatmeal cereal squares (such as Quaker Oatmeal Squares), crushed
- 1 (16 ounce) bag small pretzel rods

Directions

- Combine peanut butter and hazelnut spread thoroughly in serving bowl and add some crushed cereal squares.
- Now take out pretzel rods and dip them into this mixture to get broomsticks.
- Plate and enjoy.

Servings: 16

Timing Information:

Preparation	Cooking	Total Time
10 mins		10 mins

Nutritional Information:

Calories	291 kcal
Carbohydrates	36g
Cholesterol	0 mg
Fat	13.7 g
Protein	8.2 g
Sodium	707 mg

* Percent Daily Values are based on a 2,000 calorie diet.

Chocolate-Cinnamon Dip

Ingredients

- 1 (8 ounce) package cream cheese, softened
- 1 (7 ounce) jar marshmallow creme
- 1 (12 ounce) container frozen whipped topping, thawed
- 1 tsp ground cinnamon
- 1/2 tsp vanilla extract
- 2 1/2 tbsps chocolate-hazelnut spread, such as Nutella

Directions

- Take out a large bowl and mix cream cheese, whipped topping and marshmallow cream in a blender.
- Now add cinnamon, chocolate spread and vanilla and continuing mixing.
- Cover this dip with plastic wrap in a serving dish before refrigerating for one hour.

- Enjoy.

Servings: 6

Timing Information:

Preparation	Cooking	Total Time
10 mins		1 hr 10 mins

Nutritional Information:

Calories	90 kcal
Carbohydrates	8.8g
Cholesterol	8 mg
Fat	5.8 g
Protein	0.8 g
Sodium	31 mg

* Percent Daily Values are based on a 2,000 calorie diet.

Banana Cake

Ingredients

- 6 tbsps whole wheat flour
- 4 1/2 tbsps white sugar
- 1/8 tsp baking powder
- 1/2 banana, mashed
- 3 tbsps milk
- 3 tbsps vegetable oil
- 1 1/2 tsps vanilla extract
- 2 tbsps chocolate-hazelnut spread (such as Nutella), or to taste (optional)

Directions

- Mix flour, sugar, and baking powder together in a bowl. Stir banana, milk, oil, and vanilla extract together in a microwave-safe bowl; stir in flour mixture until batter is smooth.
- Cook in microwave until cake is cooked through, about 2 minutes. Cool slightly and spread

chocolate-hazelnut spread onto cake.

Servings: 2

Timing Information:

Preparation	Cooking	Total Time
10 mins		12 mins

Nutritional Information:

Calories	493 kcal
Carbohydrates	62.2g
Cholesterol	2 mg
Fat	25.9 g
Protein	5.2 g
Sodium	57 mg

* Percent Daily Values are based on a 2,000 calorie diet.

Delightful Nutella Sandwich

Ingredients

- 2 tbsps almond butter
- 2 slices multigrain bread
- 1 tbsp chocolate hazelnut spread
- 1/2 bananas, sliced

Directions

- Place bananas over the almond butter that is spread over 1 side of one slice and place this over the other slice of the bread which also has chocolate spread topping to make a delicious sandwich.

Servings: 11

Timing Information:

Preparation	Cooking	Total Time
10 mins	10 mins	20 mins

Nutritional Information:

Calories	473 kcal
Carbohydrates	52.3g
Cholesterol	0 mg
Fat	25.8 g
Protein	13.4 g
Sodium	378 mg

* Percent Daily Values are based on a 2,000 calorie diet.

Chocolate Spread II

Ingredients

- 1 cup unsalted butter, softened
- 3 tbsps honey, or more to taste
- 3 tbsps unsweetened cocoa powder

Directions

- Whisk butter and honey very thoroughly until both are completely mixed and add cocoa mix it well
- You can store this in the refrigerator for two weeks.

Servings: 12

Timing Information:

Preparation	Cooking	Total Time
10 mins		10 mins

Nutritional Information:

Calories	155 kcal
Carbohydrates	5.1g
Cholesterol	41 mg
Fat	15.5 g
Protein	0.4 g
Sodium	3 mg

* Percent Daily Values are based on a 2,000 calorie diet.

Peanut Butter Re-Imagined

Ingredients

- 1 (14 ounce) can sweetened condensed milk
- 1/4 cup creamy peanut butter
- 1/4 cup hazelnut-flavored syrup for beverages
- 2 tbsps honey
- 1 tsp vanilla extract
- 1 cup chocolate chips

Directions

- Put all the ingredients except chocolate chips that are mentioned into saucepan and mix it thoroughly before cooking it at medium heat for about 5 minutes.
- Remove this saucepan from the heat and add chocolate chips while stirring regularly to get it melted.

- Pour this into some jar and let it cool down.

NOTE: Use this mixture as a peanut butter replacement.

Servings: 15

Timing Information:

Preparation	Cooking	Total Time
5 mins	5 mins	40 mins

Nutritional Information:

Calories	186 kcal
Carbohydrates	28g
Cholesterol	9 mg
Fat	7.8 g
Protein	3.6 g
Sodium	56 mg

* Percent Daily Values are based on a 2,000 calorie diet.

Nutella Pudding

Ingredients

- 1/2 cup skinned hazelnuts
- 1 cup low-fat ricotta cheese
- 3 tbsps cocoa powder (such as Callebaut)
- 2 tbsps stevia powder
- 1/2 scoop vanilla whey protein powder
- 1 tsp vanilla extract

Directions

- First, preheat your oven to 375 degrees and spread hazelnuts on a baking sheet before continuing.
- Now place this baking sheet into the microwave oven for about 12 minutes and let it cool down.
- Now put hazelnuts, stevia, ricotta, cocoa power, vanilla protein powder and vanilla in the blender and blend until smooth.

Servings: 2

Timing Information:

Preparation	Cooking	Total Time
10 mins	10 mins	40 mins

Nutritional Information:

Calories	459 kcal
Carbohydrates	26.2g
Cholesterol	41 mg
Fat	31.7 g
Protein	30 g
Sodium	209 mg

* Percent Daily Values are based on a 2,000 calorie diet.

Coffee Enhanced

Ingredients

- 2 cups ice cubes
- 1 1/2 cups milk
- 3 tbsps white sugar
- 2 tbsps chocolate-hazelnut spread (such as Nutella)
- 4 tsps instant coffee granules
- 1 tbsp vanilla extract

Directions

- Put all the ingredients mentioned into a blender and blend for about 30 seconds or until the required smoothness is achieved.
- Enjoy your unique tasting coffee.

Servings: 2

Timing Information:

Preparation	Cooking	Total Time
10 mins		10 mins

Nutritional Information:

Calories	267 kcal
Carbohydrates	38.3g
Cholesterol	15 mg
Fat	8.1 g
Protein	7.3 g
Sodium	99 mg

* Percent Daily Values are based on a 2,000 calorie diet.

Maggie's Homemade Granola Crisps

Ingredients
- 1 C. raisins (optional)
- 3/4 C. unsweetened applesauce
- 3 tbsps unsweetened applesauce
- 2/3 C. chocolate-hazelnut spread
- 1/2 C. brown sugar
- 1/4 C. honey
- 2 tbsps corn syrup
- 2 tbsps vanilla extract
- 1 tbsp ground cinnamon
- 1 tbsp salt
- 3 1/3 C. old-fashioned oats
- 2/3 C. all-purpose flour

Directions
- Coat a casserole dish with oil and then set your oven to 350 degrees before doing anything else.
- Get a bowl, combine: salt, raisins, 3/4 C. and 3 tbsps of applesauce, cinnamon, hazelnut spread, vanilla, brown sugar, corn syrup,

and honey. Stir the mix until it is even and smooth.
- Get a 2nd bowl, mix: flour and oats.
- Combine both bowls and stir the contents. Now add in the granola. Then pour the mix into your casserole dish.
- Cook everything in the oven for 17 mins then let the contents cool on a rack before slicing the dessert into bars of your preferred size.
- Enjoy.

Servings: 24

Timing Information:

Preparation	Cooking	Total Time
15 m	15 m	1 h 30 m

Nutritional Information:

Calories	150 kcal
Fat	2.8 g
Carbohydrates	29.8g
Protein	2.5 g
Cholesterol	0 mg
Sodium	108 mg

* Percent Daily Values are based on a 2,000 calorie diet.

Toast from France

Ingredients
- 2 tbsps chocolate-hazelnut spread, or more to taste
- 4 slices cinnamon bread (such as Pepperidge Farm(R))
- 1/4 C. milk
- 1 large egg, beaten
- 1/4 tbsp vanilla extract
- cooking spray

Directions
- Coat 1 side of 2 pieces of bread with hazelnut spread. Then form sandwiches with the rest of the bread.
- Get a bowl, combine: vanilla, milk, and eggs. Submerge each sandwich in this mix for about 20 secs then flip the sandwich and let it sit in the mix for 20 more secs.

- Coat a skillet with nonstick spray, liberally, then for 3 mins fry the sandwiches in the skillet.
- After 2 mins of frying flip the sandwich and cook the opposite side for 1 additional min.
- Enjoy.

Servings: 2

Timing Information:

Preparation	Cooking	Total Time
10 m	5 m	15 m

Nutritional Information:

Calories	296 kcal
Fat	12.8 g
Carbohydrates	39.6g
Protein	11.2 g
Cholesterol	95 mg
Sodium	296 mg

* Percent Daily Values are based on a 2,000 calorie diet.

Choco Cookies

Ingredients
- 2 1/2 C. all-purpose flour
- 1/4 C. unsweetened cocoa powder
- 1 tbsp baking soda
- 1 tbsp salt
- 1 C. butter, room temperature
- 3/4 C. brown sugar
- 3/4 C. white sugar
- 2 large eggs
- 2 tbsps vanilla extract
- 1/2 C. chocolate-hazelnut spread
- 1/2 C. diced toasted hazelnuts
- 1 C. chocolate chips

Directions
- Coat a cookie sheet with oil then set your oven to 350 degrees before doing anything else.
- Get a bowl, combine: salt, flour, baking soda, and cocoa powder. Mix this evenly until it is completely smooth.

- Get a 2nd bowl, and with a mixer, combine: white sugar, butter, and brown sugar. Then one by one add in your eggs and continue mixing.
- After all of the eggs have been combined in add the hazelnut spread and the vanilla. Then stir the mix a few more times.
- Now gradually combine both bowls and add in the chocolate ships and the hazelnuts.
- Drop dollops of this mix on the prepared cookie sheet.
- Cook the cookies in the oven for 14 mins then let them cool on a rack for 5 mins before serving.
- Enjoy.

Servings: 12

Timing Information:

Preparation	Cooking	Total Time
30 m	12 m	57 m

Nutritional Information:

Calories	502 kcal
Fat	26.7 g
Carbohydrates	63.1g
Protein	6.1 g
Cholesterol	68 mg
Sodium	434 mg

* Percent Daily Values are based on a 2,000 calorie diet.

Hazelnut Puff Pastry Rolls

Ingredients
- 1 (8 oz.) package phyllo dough, thawed if frozen
- 1/2 C. melted butter
- 1/2 (13 oz.) jar chocolate-hazelnut spread

Directions
- Set your oven to 400 degrees before doing anything else.
- Take one piece of phyllo and coat half of it with butter then fold the opposite side over the buttered side.
- Add 1 tbsp of hazelnut spread in the center of the dough then place the rest of the butter around the rest of the dough's surface.
- Now roll this dough into a tube and layer it on a cookie sheet.
- Continue preparing the dough pieces in this manner until all the ingredients have been used up.

- Now cook them in the oven for 12 mins.
- Enjoy.

Servings: 25

Timing Information:

Preparation	Cooking	Total Time
1 h	10 m	1 h 10 m

Nutritional Information:

Calories	97 kcal
Fat	6.3 g
Carbohydrates	9.2g
Protein	1.1 g
Cholesterol	10 mg
Sodium	76 mg

* Percent Daily Values are based on a 2,000 calorie diet.

No-Bake Hazelnut Oat Bars

Ingredients
- 1 C. butter
- 2 C. white sugar
- 1 tbsp vanilla extract
- 1/4 tbsp salt
- 1 C. peanut butter
- 1 C. chocolate-hazelnut spread
- 3 C. rolled oats

Directions
- Cover a casserole dish with foil before doing anything else.
- Now begin to heat and stir the following until it is all boiling: salt, butter, vanilla, and sugar.
- Once the mix is boiling continue heating and stirring for 60 secs.
- Now lower the heat to a medium level and combine in the hazelnut spread and the peanut butter.
- Continue heating and stirring for 6 mins then shut the heat and add in your oats.

- Stir the oats into the mix and pour everything into your casserole dish.
- Evenly layer the mix throughout the casserole dish with a spoon.
- Now let the mix set for 40 mins.
- Remove the foil from the casserole dish and slice the oat mix into bars of your preferred sized.
- Enjoy.

Servings: 30

Timing Information:

Preparation	Cooking	Total Time
10 m	10 m	50 m

Nutritional Information:

Calories	230 kcal
Fat	13.4 g
Carbohydrates	25.6g
Protein	3.8 g
Cholesterol	16 mg
Sodium	111 mg

* Percent Daily Values are based on a 2,000 calorie diet.

Upstate New York Style Crepes

Ingredients
- 1 C. milk
- 4 large eggs
- 1 tbsp butter, melted
- 1 tbsp white sugar
- 1 tbsp almond extract
- 1 1/4 C. all-purpose flour
- 12 slices bacon
- 3 tbsps butter, or as needed - divided
- 6 firm bananas, sliced in half lengthwise
- 12 tbsps chocolate-hazelnut spread , divided
- 12 tbsps peanut butter, divided
- 1/2 tbsp honey, divided
- 1 tbsp confectioners' sugar for dusting, or as needed
- 1 tbsp chocolate syrup, or as needed

Directions

- Process the following with a blender or food processor until smooth: flour, milk, almond extract, 1 tbsp butter, and white sugar.
- Let this mix sit for 25 mins then begin to fry your bacon, until crispy, for 12 mins then remove the excess oils.
- Now melt 1 tbsp of butter in a large frying pan and begin to fry 1/4 C. of batter for 3 mins then jiggle the pan and flip the crepe.
- Fry the opposite for 2 mins then place the crepe on a plate.
- Continue cooking crepes in this manner and add more butter to the pan to keep it coated.
- Once all your crepes are cooked add 2 more tbsp of butter to the pan and begin to fry your banana, until browned, for about 3 to 4 mins per side.
- Plate one crepe for serving and top it with 1 tbsp of hazelnut spread, 1 tbsp of peanut butter, 1

piece of bacon in the middle, and a half of a banana.
- Finally add half a tsp of honey over everything.
- Top the dish with some confectioner's and some chocolate syrup.
- Shape the crepe into a cylinder and place it in a casserole dish.
- Continue forming crepes in this manner until all of the ingredients have been used up.
- Enjoy.

Servings: 12

Timing Information:

Preparation	Cooking	Total Time
30 m	45 m	1 h 15 m

Nutritional Information:

Calories	406 kcal
Fat	22.8 g
Carbohydrates	40.3g
Protein	13.3 g
Cholesterol	84 mg
Sodium	362 mg

* Percent Daily Values are based on a 2,000 calorie diet.

Pretzel Cookies

Ingredients
- 2 C. all-purpose flour
- 2 tbsps all-purpose flour
- 1/2 tbsp baking soda
- 1/2 tbsp salt
- 1 C. brown sugar
- 1/2 C. unsalted butter, melted and cooled slightly
- 1 egg
- 1 egg yolk
- 2 tbsps natural peanut butter (such as Natural Jif(R))
- 2 tbsps vanilla extract
- 53 pretzel sticks, crushed
- 3 tbsps chocolate-hazelnut spread

Directions
- Set your oven to 350 degrees before doing anything else.
- Get a bowl, combine: salt, 2 C. and 2 tbsps of flour, and baking soda.

- Get a 2nd bowl, combine: butter and sugar.
- Then add in vanilla, eggs, peanut butter, and egg yolks.
- Now combine both bowls gradually, then add the hazelnut spread and the pretzels.
- Grab two spoons and drop dollops of the mix onto a cookie sheet and cook everything in the oven for 10 mins.
- Spin your cookie sheet and cook the cookies for 6 more mins.
- Now let the cookies cool on a rack for 10 mins.
- Enjoy.

Servings: 26

Timing Information:

Preparation	Cooking	Total Time
15 m	15 m	35 m

Nutritional Information:

Calories	239 kcal
Fat	6.2 g
Carbohydrates	41.8g
Protein	4.6 g
Cholesterol	24 mg
Sodium	604 mg

* Percent Daily Values are based on a 2,000 calorie diet.

Easy Smores

Ingredients
- 2 tbsps salted butter, softened, divided
- 1 tbsp olive oil, divided
- 4 slices 12-grain bread
- 2 tbsps peanut butter
- 2 tbsps marshmallow crème, or to taste
- 2 tbsps chocolate-hazelnut spread

Directions
- Coat 1 side of each piece of bread with 1.5 tsp olive oil and 1 tbsp of butter.
- Now add 1.5 tsps of olive oil and 1 tbsp of butter to a skillet and get it hot.
- On the non-oiled side of each piece of bread layer the following: hazelnut spread, marshmallow crème, and peanut butter.
- Form sandwiches with the oil sides facing outwards.

- Fry your sandwiches for 40 secs per side in the hot pan.
- Enjoy.

Servings: 2

Timing Information:

Preparation	Cooking	Total Time
10 m	5 m	15 m

Nutritional Information:

Calories	494 kcal
Fat	33.2 g
Carbohydrates	40g
Protein	12.2 g
Cholesterol	31 mg
Sodium	395 mg

* Percent Daily Values are based on a 2,000 calorie diet.

Sweet Cookies

Ingredients
- 1/2 C. unsalted butter at room temperature
- 3/4 C. chocolate-hazelnut spread
- 1/2 C. white sugar
- 2/3 C. packed brown sugar
- 1 egg
- 1 egg yolk
- 1/2 tbsp vanilla extract
- 2 3/4 C. all-purpose flour
- 3/4 tbsp baking soda
- 1/4 tbsp salt

Directions
- Get a bowl, and combine the following with a mixer: brown sugar, butter, white sugar, and hazelnut spread.
- Now combine in the egg and add the vanilla and egg yolks.
- Get a 2nd bowl, combine: salt, flour, and baking soda.

- Slowly combine both bowls while continuing to stir everything.
- Shape the dough into a large ball and cover the dough in plastic.
- Place the ball in a 3rd bowl and put everything in the fridge for 40 mins.
- Now set your oven to 400 degrees before doing anything else.
- Take your dough and form it into multiple large balls then place them on a baking sheet and flatten the dough balls.
- Cook the cookies in the oven for 9 mins then let them cool before serving.
- Enjoy.

Servings: 12

Timing Information:

Preparation	Cooking	Total Time
15 m	10 m	55 m

Nutritional Information:

Calories	341 kcal
Fat	13.2 g
Carbohydrates	51.8g
Protein	4.7 g
Cholesterol	51 mg
Sodium	153 mg

* Percent Daily Values are based on a 2,000 calorie diet.

Maggie's Favorite Hazelnut Cupcakes

Ingredients
- 2 C. white sugar
- 1 C. all-purpose flour
- 3/4 C. ground toasted hazelnuts
- 3/4 C. unsweetened cocoa powder
- 1 1/2 tbsps baking powder
- 1 1/2 tbsps baking soda
- 1 tbsp salt
- 2 eggs
- 1/2 C. vegetable oil
- 1 C. milk
- 2 tbsps vanilla extract
- 1/3 C. water
- 2 C. chocolate-hazelnut spread
- 1 C. diced toasted hazelnuts

Directions
- Coat a muffin tin or 18 muffin C. with oil then set your oven to 350 degrees before doing anything else.

- Get a bowl, combine: salt, sugar, baking soda, flour, baking powder, ground hazelnut nuts, and cocoa.
- Get a 2nd bowl, combine, with a mixer, until smooth: vanilla, eggs, milk, and veggie oil.
- Combine both bowls gradually then add in the water and continue stirring.
- Evenly divide the mix between your muffin sections.
- Now cook everything in the oven for 15 mins.
- Let the muffins cool for 15 mins before topping them with the hazelnut spread.
- Enjoy.

Servings: 18

Timing Information:

Preparation	Cooking	Total Time
25 m	15 m	1 h 40 m

Nutritional Information:

Calories	391 kcal
Fat	21.2 g
Carbohydrates	48.8g
Protein	5.8 g
Cholesterol	22 mg
Sodium	316 mg

* Percent Daily Values are based on a 2,000 calorie diet.

Truffle and Hazelnut Desserts

Ingredients
- 2 1/4 C. all-purpose flour
- 1/2 C. unsweetened cocoa powder
- 1 tbsp baking powder
- 3/4 C. milk
- 1/4 C. hazelnut liqueur
- 1 tbsp vanilla extract
- 1 C. butter
- 1 1/2 C. white sugar
- 3 eggs
- 24 chocolate-hazelnut truffles (such as Ferrero Rocher(R))
- 1 (13 oz.) jar chocolate-hazelnut spread
- 1/4 C. diced hazelnuts

Directions
- Cover your muffin C. or a muffin tin with foil liners or parchment paper and then set your oven to 350 degrees before doing anything else.

- Get a bowl, sift: baking powder, flour, and cocoa.
- Get a 2nd bowl, combine: vanilla, liqueur, and milk.
- Get a 3rd bowl, combine, with a mixer: sugar and butter. Then one by one add in your eggs and continue mixing.
- As you continue to mix gradually add in your flour mix and the milk mix.
- Stir the new mix to get everything smooth.
- Now add about half a C. of mix to each muffin section then put a truffle into each section of batter.
- Once you have added your unwrapped truffles add more batter.
- Cook the Cupcakes in the oven for 23 mins then let the cupcakes cool for 15 mins.
- Coat each dessert with some hazelnut spread.
- Enjoy.

Servings: 24

Timing Information:

Preparation	Cooking	Total Time
20 m	25 m	45 m

Nutritional Information:

Calories	345 kcal
Fat	18.9 g
Carbohydrates	39.3g
Protein	5.2 g
Cholesterol	44 mg
Sodium	135 mg

* Percent Daily Values are based on a 2,000 calorie diet.

Pancakes from Denmark

Ingredients
- 1 C. whole wheat flour
- 2 tbsps white sugar
- 2 1/2 tbsps baking powder
- 1/2 tbsp salt
- 1/4 tbsp ground cinnamon
- 1 dash ground nutmeg
- 7 tsps chocolate hazel nut spread
- 1 dash ground cloves
- 1 egg, lightly beaten
- 3/4 C. milk
- 2 tbsps unsalted butter, melted
- 1 tbsp vanilla extract

Directions
- Get a bowl, combine: cloves, flour, nutmeg, sugar, cinnamon, baking powder, and salt. Then combine in: vanilla, egg, butter, and milk.
- Get your Aebleskiver pan hot and then coat it with non-stick spray.

- Ladle the batter into each section and leave about 1/3 of space.
- Now cook the batter for 4 mins then use a skewer to turn the muffin by ¼ of a turn.
- Continue this turning process every few mins until everything is cooked.
- Top each of your muffins with 1 tsp of hazelnut spread before serving.
- Enjoy.

Servings: 7

Timing Information:

Preparation	Cooking	Total Time
5 m	5 m	10 m

Nutritional Information:

Calories	127 kcal
Fat	4.8 g
Carbohydrates	18g
Protein	4.1 g
Cholesterol	34 mg
Sodium	362 mg

* Percent Daily Values are based on a 2,000 calorie diet.

Strawberry Hazelnut Bark

Ingredients
- 3 C. strawberries, stemmed and quartered
- 4 C. dark chocolate chips, melted
- 3 C. peanut butter, melted
- 3 C. chocolate-hazelnut spread, melted
- 2 C. marshmallow cream (such as Marshmallow Fluff(R)), melted

Directions
- Cover a cookie sheet with parchment paper.
- Get a bowl and add in your strawberries.
- Grab a potato masher and puree the strawberries.
- Combine in: marshmallow cream, melted chocolate, hazelnut spread, and peanut butter.
- Now pour this mix onto your cookie sheet.

- Place the contents in the fridge for 60 mins.
- Enjoy.

Servings: 45

Timing Information:

Preparation	Cooking	Total Time
15 m		1 h 15 m

Nutritional Information:

Calories	276 kcal
Fat	17.5 g
Carbohydrates	28.2g
Protein	6.3 g
Cholesterol	0 mg
Sodium	103 mg

* Percent Daily Values are based on a 2,000 calorie diet.

Two Times Chocolate Cookies

Ingredients
- 1/2 C. butter, at room temperature
- 3/4 C. white sugar
- 1/4 tbsp salt
- 1 egg
- 1 tbsp vanilla extract
- 1 3/4 oz. 70% dark chocolate, melted
- 1 tbsp cocoa powder
- 1/4 tbsp instant espresso powder (optional)
- 1 C. all-purpose flour
- 1/2 C. semisweet chocolate chips
- 1/2 C. roasted hazelnuts, diced
- 1/4 C. roasted hazelnuts, finely ground
- 4 tbsps hazelnut spread

Directions
- Cover two cookie sheets with parchment paper and then set

your oven to 325 degrees before doing anything else.
- With an electric mixer, mix your butter until fluffy, in a bowl. Then combine in salt and sugar.
- Continue mixing then add in the vanilla, eggs, expresso, melted chocolate, and cocoa.
- Mix the contents for 60 secs before adding the flour in slowly.
- Once the mix is smooth add the ground and diced hazelnuts and also the chocolate chips.
- Drop dollops of the mix onto the cookie sheets and flatten them with a spoon.
- Cook the cookies in the oven for 15 mins then let them cool for 10 mins before serving and topping each one with some hazelnut spread.
- Enjoy.

Servings: 24

Timing Information:

Preparation	Cooking	Total Time
25 m	15 m	40 m

Nutritional Information:

Calories	133 kcal
Fat	8.3 g
Carbohydrates	14.3g
Protein	1.6 g
Cholesterol	18 mg
Sodium	82 mg

* Percent Daily Values are based on a 2,000 calorie diet.

Hazelnut Peanut Butter Sandwiches

Ingredients
- 6 slices sandwich bread
- 3/4 C. peanut butter
- 3/4 C. chocolate-hazelnut spread

Directions
- Take your pieces of bread, remove the crusts, and then toast them.
- Coat twelve pieces of bread with peanut butter and then coat the other pieces of bread with the chocolate hazelnut spread.
- Form a sandwich from one slice with peanut butter and one slice with hazelnut spread.
- Enjoy.

Servings: 6

Timing Information:

Preparation	Cooking	Total Time
10 m	5 m	15 m

Nutritional Information:

Calories	416 kcal
Fat	26.1 g
Carbohydrates	38g
Protein	12 g
Cholesterol	0 mg
Sodium	348 mg

* Percent Daily Values are based on a 2,000 calorie diet.

Thanks for Reading! Now Let's Try some Sushi and Dump Dinners....

Send the Book!

To grab this **box set** simply follow the link mentioned above, or tap the book cover.

This will take you to a page where you can simply enter your email address and a PDF version of the **box set** will be emailed to you.

I hope you are ready for some serious cooking!

[Send the Book!](#)

You will also receive updates about all my new books when they are free.

Also don't forget to like and subscribe on the social networks. I love meeting my readers. Links to all my profiles are below so please click and connect :)

[Facebook](#)

[Twitter](#)

Come On...
Let's Be Friends :)

I adore my readers and love connecting with them socially. Please follow the links below so we can connect on Facebook, Twitter, and Google+.

Facebook

Twitter

I also have a blog that I regularly update for my readers so check it out below.

My Blog

About The Publisher.

BookSumo specializes in providing the best books on special topics that you care about. *The Easy Nutella Cookbook* will teach you the most amazing uses of Nutella.

To find out more about BookSumo and find other books we have written go to:

http://booksumo.com/.

CAN I ASK A FAVOUR?

If you found this book interesting, or have otherwise found any benefit in it. Then may I ask that you post a review of it on Amazon? Nothing excites me more than new reviews, especially reviews which suggest new topics for writing. I do read all reviews and I always factor feedback into my newer works.

So if you are willing to take ten minutes to write what you sincerely thought about this book then please visit our Amazon page and post your opinions.

Again thank you!

INTERESTED IN OTHER EASY COOKBOOKS?

Everything is easy! Check out my Amazon Author page for more great cookbooks:

For a complete listing of all my books please see my author page.

Made in the USA
Lexington, KY
23 November 2017